The Environment

SCIENCE NEWS for KIDS

Computers and Technology

Earth Science

The Environment

Food and Nutrition

Health and Medicine

Space and Astronomy

The Environment

Series Editor
Tara Koellhoffer

With a Foreword by
Emily Sohn,
Science News for Kids

CHELSEA
CLUBHOUSE
An Imprint of Chelsea House Publishers

The Environment

Chelsea Clubhouse
An imprint of Chelsea House Publishers
132 West 31st Street
New York NY 10001

For Library of Congress Cataloging-in-Publication Data, please contact the
publisher.

ISBN 0-7910-9123-6

Chelsea House books are available at special discounts when purchased in
bulk quantities for businesses, associations, institutions, or sales promotions.
Please call our Special Sales Department in New York at (212) 967-8800 or
(800) 322-8755.

You can find Chelsea House on the World Wide Web at
http://www.chelseahouse.com

Text and cover design by Takeshi Takahashi
Layout by Ladybug Editorial & Design

Printed in the United States of America

Bang   10 9 8 7 6 5 4 3 2 1

This book is printed on acid-free paper.

All links, web addresses, and Internet search terms were checked and verified
to be correct at the time of publication. Because of the dynamic nature of the
web, some addresses and links may have changed since publication and may
no longer be valid.

Contents Overview

Detailed Table of Contents

by Emily Sohn
Science News for Kids

Science, for many kids, is just another subject in school. You may have biology tests and astronomy quizzes to study for, chemistry formulas to memorize, physics problems to work through, or current events to report on. All of it, after a while, can seem like a major drag.

Now, forget about all that, and think about your day. What did you eat for breakfast? How did you get to school and what did you think about along the way? What makes the room bright enough for you to see this book? How does the room stay cool or warm enough for you to be comfortable? What do you like to do for fun?

All of your answers, in some way, involve science. Food, transportation, electricity, toys, video games, animals, plants, your brain, the rest of your body: Behind the scenes of nearly anything you can think of, there are scientists trying to figure out how it works, how it came to be, or how to make it better. Science can explain why pizza and chocolate taste good. Science gives airplanes a lift. And science is behind the medicines that make your aches and pains go away. Most exciting of all, science never stands still.

Science News for Kids tracks the trends and delves into the discoveries that make life more interesting and more efficient every day. The stories in these volumes explore a tiny fraction of the grand scope of research happening around the world. These stories point out the questions that push scientists to probe ever deeper into physics, chemistry, biology, psychology, and more. Reading about the challenges of science will spark in you the same sort of curiosity that drives researchers to keep searching for answers, despite setbacks and failed experiments. The stories here may even inspire you to seek out your own solutions to the world's puzzles.

Being a scientist is hard work, but it can be one of the best jobs around. You may picture scientists always tinkering away in their labs, pouring chemicals into flasks and reading technical papers. Well, they do those things some of the time. But they also get to dig around in the dirt, blow things up, and even ride rockets into outer space. They travel around the world. They save lives. And, they get to spend most of their time thinking about the things that fascinate them most, all in the name of work.

Sometimes, researchers have revelations that change the way we think about the universe. Albert Einstein, for one, explained light, space, time, and other aspects of the physical world in radically new terms. He's perhaps the most famous scientist in history, thanks to his theories of relativity and other ideas. Likewise, James Watson and

Francis Crick forever changed the face of medicine when they first described the structure of the genetic material DNA in 1953. Today, doctors use information about DNA to explain why some people are likely to develop certain diseases and why others may have trouble reading or doing math. Police investigators rely on DNA to solve mysteries when they analyze hairs, blood, saliva, and remains at the scene of a crime. And scientists are now eagerly pursuing potential uses of DNA to cure cancer and other diseases.

Science can be about persistence and courage as much as it is about grand ideas. Society doesn't always welcome new ideas. Before Galileo Galilei became one of the first people to point a telescope at the sky in the early 1600s, for example, nearly everyone believed that the planets revolved around Earth. Galileo discovered four moons orbiting Jupiter. He saw that Venus has phases, like the moon. And he noticed spots on the sun and lumps on the moon's craggy face. All of these observations shook up the widely held view that the heavens were perfect, orderly, and centered on Earth. Galileo's ideas were so controversial, in fact, that he was forced to deny them to save his life. Even then, he was sentenced to imprisonment in his own home.

Since Galileo's time, the public has so completely accepted his views of the universe that space missions have been named after him, as have craters on the moon and on Mars. In 1969, Neil Armstrong became the first person to stand on the moon. Now, astronauts spend months in orbit, living on an international space station, floating in weightlessness. Spacecraft have landed on planets and moons as far away as Saturn. One probe recently slammed into a comet to collect information. With powerful telescopes, astronomers continue to spot undiscovered moons in our solar system, planets orbiting stars in other parts of our galaxy, and evidence of the strange behavior of black holes. New technologies continue to push the limits of what we can detect in outer space and what we know about how the universe formed.

Here on Earth, computer technology has transformed society in a short period of time. The first electronic digital computers, which appeared in the 1940s, took up entire rooms and weighed thousands of pounds. Decades passed before people started using their own PCs (personal computers) at home. Laptops came even later.

These days, it's hard to imagine life without computers. They track restaurant orders. They help stores process credit cards. They allow you to play video games, send e-mails and instant messages to your friends, and write reports that you can edit and print without ever picking up a pen. Doctors use computers to diagnose their patients, and banks use computers to keep track of our money. As computers become more and more popular, they continue to get smaller, more powerful, less expensive, and more integrated into our lives in ways we don't even notice.

Probes that fly to Pluto and computers the size of peas are major advances that don't happen overnight. Science is a process of small steps, and a new discovery often starts with a single question. Why, for example, do hurricanes and tsunamis form? What is it like at the center of Earth? Why do some types of french fries taste better than others? Research projects can also begin with observations. There are fewer tigers in India than there used to be, for instance. Kids now weigh more than they did a generation ago. Mars shows signs that the planet once supported life.

The next step is investigation, which can take on many forms, depending on the subject. Brain researchers, for one, often do experiments in their laboratories with the help of sophisticated equipment. In one type of neuroscience study, subjects repeatedly solve tasks while machines measure activity in their brains. Some environmental scientists who study climate, on the other hand, collect data by tracking weather patterns over the years. Paleontologists dig deep into the earth to look for clues about what the world was like when dinosaurs were alive. Anthropologists learn about other cultures by talking to people and collecting stories. Doctors monitor large numbers of patients taking a new drug or no drug to figure out whether a drug is safe and effective before others can use it.

Designing studies requires creativity, and scientists spend many years training to use the tools of their profession. Physicists need to learn complicated mathematical formulas. Ecologists make models that simulate interactions between species. Physicians learn the name of every bone and blood vessel in the body. The most basic tools, however, are ones that everyone has: our senses. The best way to start learning about the world through science is to pay attention to what you smell, taste, see, hear, and feel. Notice. Ask questions. Collect data. Do experiments. Draw tentative conclusions. Ask more questions.

Most importantly, leave no stone unturned. There's no limit to the topics available for research. Robots, computers, and new technologies in medicine are the waves of the future. Just as important, however, are studies of the past. Figuring out what Earth's climate used to be like and which animals and plants used to live here are the first steps toward understanding how the planet is changing and what those changes might mean for our future. And don't forget to look around at what's going on around you, right now. You might just be surprised at how many subjects you can find to investigate.

Ready to get started? The stories in this book are great sources of inspiration. Each of the articles comes directly from the *Science News for Kids* Website, which you can find online at *http://sciencenewsforkids.org*. All articles at the site, which is updated weekly, cover current events in science, and all are written with middle-school students in mind. If anything you read in this book sparks your interest, feel free to visit the Website to check out the latest developments and find out more.

And keep an eye out for an occasional feature called "News Detective." These essays describe what it's like to be a science journalist, roaming the world in search of scientists at work. Science writing is an often-overlooked career possibility, but science writers have endless opportunities to learn about many things at once, to share in the excitement of scientific discovery, and to help scientists get the word out about the significance of their work.

So, go ahead and turn the page. There's so much left to discover.

Section 1

Conservation

For hundreds of years, people spent more time pursuing profits than worrying about the effects they were having on the land around them. As a result, in many industrialized countries, the amount of empty, undeveloped land is limited, and what is left is often polluted. We are also running dangerously short of potential fuel sources, as we continue to rely on oil and other fossil fuels to power our cars, trucks, and factories.

Over the last century, and especially within the last few decades, environmentalists have taken steps to try to save our remaining wilderness and to find ways to conserve energy. In this section, we examine some of the most pressing issues related to conservation and the environment, and the programs that have been put in place to try to save our world. From protecting the wetlands that serve as habitats for birds, fish, and other water-loving creatures to putting out the devastating wildfires that destroy massive chunks of forest in Yellowstone Park and other sites in the western United States, the conservation effort is diverse—and critical for our future survival.

—The Editor

Protecting the Vanishing Wetlands

Whether marshes or mangroves, swamps or bayous, wetlands provide a unique habitat for some of the most unusual species of animals on Earth. Migrating birds, alligators, and frogs are just some of the creatures that make the wetlands their home. Unfortunately, for various reasons—from global climate change to industrial development—the wetlands are rapidly disappearing. In the following article, author Emily Sohn looks at the valuable wetlands and the steps scientists are taking to try to protect them.

—The Editor

Saving Wetlands

by Emily Sohn

Before Reading:

- **Why is it important to protect different ecosystems?**

- **Where would you find wetlands?**

There's water, and there's land. Somewhere in the middle, there are wetlands.

Not totally flooded by water, but not completely dry either, these in-between places rank among the richest **ecosystems** on Earth. Marshes, mangroves, bogs, swamps, bayous, prairie potholes, and other wetlands often have more plant and animal life than any lakes, rivers, grasslands, forests, or hillsides nearby.

Baby fish and shellfish thrive in the protected waters of shallow **estuaries**, where rivers meet the sea. Many types of migratory birds spend their winters in marshes or stop there to rest during their travels (Figure 1.1). Wetlands are full of salamanders, frogs, turtles, snakes, and alligators, as well as sea grasses and other specialized plants.

"They're really beautiful environments," says Denise

Figure 1.1 Wetlands like this serve as permanent or seasonal homes for millions of birds, fish, and other animals.

Reed of the University of New Orleans. She studies landforms and the processes that made them.

Reed is determined to get people to care about wetlands—and not just because they're beautiful.

Wetlands also help preserve water quality. They protect land from getting battered by storms. And they fuel billions of dollars' worth of recreation, fisheries, and other industries.

- What is an estuary, and why is it important?

DISAPPEARING MARSHES

Unfortunately, the world's wetlands are disappearing.

In the last few hundred years, more than half of the wetlands in the United States (excluding Alaska and Hawaii) have vanished, according to the National Wetlands Research Center. The center is part of the U.S. Geological Survey.

Louisiana's wetlands, in particular, are in need of help. Even though it's a fairly small state, Louisiana holds 30% of the nation's coastal marshes along its meandering coastline, especially where the Mississippi River drains into the Gulf of Mexico.

Yet, of all marshes that have disappeared in the United States, 90% were in Louisiana, according to an organization known as America's Wetland. This group is dedicated to saving the Louisiana coast.

During the 20th century, 1.2 million acres [485,623 hectares] of land were lost along the state's coast. Between 1990 and 2000 alone, the equivalent of a foot-ball field–sized area of wetland disappeared every 38 minutes.

These are more than just numbers. As wetlands vanish, fish and migrating birds lose critical habitat. Some of these species are already endangered.

Human lives are at stake, too. More than half of Louisiana's population lives along the water, and many of these people rely on fishing and shipping to survive.

"I think it's one of the biggest environmental issues there is," says Garret Graves. Graves grew up in Louisiana but now lives in Washington, D.C., where he works with Louisiana politicians to create laws that will help restore the area.

- **What makes Louisiana an especially important place to consider in the disappearance of wetlands?**

VANISHING MYSTERY

Why Louisiana's wetlands have been disappearing has long puzzled researchers. Now, after several decades of research, some of the reasons are becoming clearer.

The culprit isn't normal erosion, which happens when waves gnaw away at the land. In this case, the marshes are falling apart from the inside out.

Walking through the wetlands used to be like slogging through a squishy field of wet hay. Now, invisible holes lie all over the place. People walking around in the marshes today can fall up to their knees in water without warning, Reed says. "It's like a Swiss cheese effect."

Why this is happening is a complicated question. There seem to be a number of factors involved, Reed says.

One is the Mississippi River. Water used to come

down the Mississippi full of **sediment** and dirt, which piled up in the marshes and kept them sturdy. Flooding was part of the normal course of things, and the process helped distribute sediment.

Then, in the mid-1900s, oil companies discovered a huge quantity of oil and gas just off the coast of Louisiana. They built extensive networks of canals, called levees, to control the flow of the river, providing better access to Earth's natural resources. These efforts ended up changing the flooding cycle. Sediment couldn't spread through the marshes, and the wetlands grew weaker.

Next came development, which filled in marshes to build parking lots, shopping centers, and houses on top of the wetlands.

Large rat-like animals called **nutrias** are also causing problems. In a healthy marsh, the animals simply graze year after year without causing too much damage. When a marsh is stressed out, though, nutrias eat away at them.

All these stresses add up. "There's no one factor you can point to and say, 'This is the culprit. Here's the smoking gun,'" Reed says. "There are many things going on that cause stress to wetlands. The wetlands could take any one or two of them. Once you get three or four on top of each other, though, the marsh just can't hang on anymore."

TRAPPING SEDIMENT

> • How has development affected wetlands?

Now that scientists have a good idea of what's happening to the wetlands, the next challenge is to figure out how to fix the problem, Reed says.

In her research, she's trying to understand why some marshes have managed to survive, even as so many others have vanished.

"How do they keep their heads above water?" she asks. "Where do they get their sediment from? How do they build themselves up when the land is subsiding?"

For about 10 years, Reed has been scattering sediment traps made out of filter paper on the surface of marshes in Louisiana. She attaches the traps to the ground with aluminum wire. Then, she checks them every two weeks.

The traps are clean when Reed puts them in and muddy when she comes back. With the data she collects, she can track when and how much sediment builds up over short periods of time and over the years. She also takes samples of the soil to study how plant roots might help hold a wetland together.

Among her results, Reed has found that hurricanes actually deposit a lot of sediment in salt-water marshes. "Everyone thinks 'Hurricanes, oh my God, they're so bad,'" Reed says. "It is bad for people. For marshes, it keeps them going."

POLITICAL ACTION

Even as research continues to help scientists understand what wetlands need, understanding can go only so far, Graves says. The only way to truly reverse wetland destruction, he argues, is through politics.

It would cost $15 billion to cut slits in the earth and restore natural sediment flow patterns along the Louisiana coast, Graves says. That's money the state doesn't have. He wants the U.S. Congress to create new laws that would give Louisiana a big chunk of the profits that come from the oil and gas obtained off its coast.

The state could then put this money toward reconstructing the environment. Right now, the U.S. government officially owns these resources.

- **What could the U.S. federal government do to help reverse wetland destruction?**

Despite eight years of work on the issue, Graves hasn't seen much progress. His passion has grown with his frustration.

Scientists and politicians aren't the only ones who have grown passionate about Louisiana's wetlands. Kids have started to get involved, too.

In early 2005, an educational program called the JASON Expedition gave middle school students a close look at wetland research in Louisiana.

Most of the students participated in the expedition

through the Internet and live **satellite** broadcasts, but some actually got to dig in the mud and explore the science with their own hands.

By the end of the weeklong program, the most popular question from kids, Reed says, was, "What can I do?"

The answer, she says, depends on where you're from. You may not live in Louisiana or even near a coast. Chances are, though, Louisiana's problems hit closer to home than you might think.

NEARBY WETLANDS

"Almost everyone has a wetlands nearby," Reed says. If you're looking for a science fair project idea, she suggests, go find out about your local wetlands.

"As you learn and understand it better, you might then see things you can do in terms of cleaning it up," she says. "Learning is part of doing something. Try to understand how it works."

Find out what sustains the wetlands in your area, why they're there, and what they give to your community. Think about the water that drains into them, where it comes from, and what you can do to keep it clean.

Using less water is something everyone can do, Reed says. This helps keep rivers and lakes full, which reduces the strain on wetlands. Paying attention to what goes down storm drains can protect them, too.

If you're really inspired, you can study to become a wetland **ecologist**. Wetlands are fascinating systems to study, Reed says, because they're always changing.

When the fish are jumping, the birds singing, and the marshes green, wetlandscapes can be beautiful. Even better, they're full of mud, and studying them requires hands-on slogging through squishy dirt and mud, Reed says. "Who doesn't like getting dirty?"

Whatever we do, it's important to do it soon, she adds. "This system could be in radically different shape in 10 years if we get moving," she says. "If we stay this way, it's still going to be in radically different shape, but in the wrong direction."

• **Name something that you could do in your own community to help save wetlands.**

After Reading:

- Why do you think that wetlands are home to so many different plants and animals?

- Design an experiment that you could do to study some aspect of a wetland ecosystem.

- Why do you think that many people might not be as concerned about saving wetlands as they are about other environmental issues?

- Who should help pay for restoring wetlands in Louisiana? Why?

- Natural disasters such as hurricanes, volcanoes, and forest fires can play important roles in ecosystems. If you could stop hurricanes from happening, would that be a good idea? Why or why not?

Looking at Lake Tanganyika

Lake Tanganyika is Africa's second largest lake. It lies in eastern-central Africa on the borders of Tanzania, Zambia, Congo, and Burundi. In large lakes like this one, heat tends to rise to the surface, while nutrients sink to the bottom. This can be a big problem for the living things that make the lake their home. In the following article, author Emily Sohn looks at what changing lake temperatures mean for water life as they dramatically affect the food chain and possibly lead some species to extinction.

—The Editor

Less Mixing Can Affect Lake's Ecosystem

by Emily Sohn

Lakes can be like bowls of soup in the microwave: They need a little stirring every now and then. Otherwise, all the heat ends up on top.

That's exactly what's happened in recent years to Africa's Lake Tanganyika, scientists are reporting. Rising water temperatures have interfered with the lake's normal mixing. As a result, the tiny organisms at the base of the food chain aren't as abundant as they used to be.

Lake Tanganyika is the second-largest body of fresh water in the world, after Lake Baikal in Russia (Figure 1.2). The African lake is more than 1 kilometer [0.62 miles] deep in some places.

In such a large lake, nutrients tend to sink to the bottom. That's bad news for the **microorganisms** called **plankton**, which live near the surface. Normally, these microscopic creatures rely on winds to churn the lake water and bring valuable nutrients back up.

But times have changed. Since 1913, the water temperature at the bottom of Lake Tanganyika has risen by about 0.2 Celsius degrees [32.4°F]. Water near the surface has warmed by almost a full degree. Cold water is

Figure 1.2 Lake Tanganyika in eastern-central Africa is the second-largest body of fresh water in the world.

more dense than warm water, so the lake has grown more resistant to mixing.

With smaller amounts of nutrients coming up to the surface, the tiny creatures are suffering. Researchers found that populations of several species of plankton dropped 70% from 1975 to 2001.

Scientists are worried because plankton are at the base of the **food chain** in lake ecosystems. So if plankton disappear, bigger creatures may run out of food and die out, too.

Waves of extinction, if they continue, could be far worse than burning your tongue on an unevenly heated bowl of chili.

Going Deeper:

Perkins, Sid. "Slow Turnover: Warming Trend Affects African Ecosystem." *Science News* 163 (June 28, 2003): 404–405. Available online at *http://www.sciencenews.org/20030628/fob4.asp*.

Wildfire

Every summer, it seems like the news is filled with stories about devastating wildfires sweeping through parts of the American West, destroying huge swathes of trees and homes and either killing wildlife or ruining their habitats. In places where drought occurs regularly, wildfire is a serious problem. As author Emily Sohn explains in the following article, some people devote their lives and careers to watching out for wildfires, serving as a vital early warning system to help firefighters and government officials respond at the first sign that a fire is threatening. Through their efforts, it may be possible to save the forests—and the animals that live in them.

—The Editor

Watching for Wildfires in Yellowstone

by Emily Sohn

Before Reading:

- What is the first image that comes to mind when you think of Yellowstone National Park?

- What are some causes of forest fires? What other things, besides trees, are harmed when wildfires break out?

- Why might the park service station a ranger to look out from a mountaintop? What are some of the things that such a firewatcher might see?

I hiked for 5 hours to reach a remote mountaintop in Wyoming in the summer of 2003. George Henley had already been there for 22 seasons.

Every summer, George spends 3 months living in a one-room cabin on top of Mount Holmes, a 10,330-foot [3,149-m] peak in the northwest corner of Yellowstone National Park.

By day, he looks for fires, takes weather readings, and talks to the rare hiker who makes the rigorous 9.6-mile [15.5-km] trek to his hut. At night, he stokes a wood-burning stove and hunkers down against cold winds.

20

Every few weeks, a helicopter delivers groceries, firewood, and propane fuel. He sometimes goes two or three weeks without seeing anyone.

"It gets lonely," George says. "It's the same view I see for years and years. I get tired of it sometimes. I sit here and think, 'I'll get out of here some day.'"

Luckily, he hasn't left yet.

George is an important link in a national fire and weather reporting system, says Roy Renkin, a vegetation management specialist at Yellowstone.

Like George, other rangers are stationed at strategic vantage points in parks and on public lands all around the country. They keep records of wind, temperature, and

• **What does George Henley do for a living?**

humidity. They notice changes in the animals that show up from year to year. And, perhaps most important of all, at least in Yellowstone, they look for fires.

"They call in these smokes very quickly, before many people have a chance to see them," Renkin says, referring to Yellowstone's three firewatchers. "With the work they do, we're able to initiate fire-management activities very soon after the fire gets observed."

Wildfires flare up every summer all over the western United States. The summer of 2003 was especially dry in many areas, and numerous fires continued to blaze in

California, Montana, Wyoming, and other states.

Experts disagree on how best to handle the blazes. Flames destroy property. They kill plants, animals, sometimes even people (Figure 1.3). Yet research continues to show that fire is a natural part of life. Entire ecosystems, in fact, may depend on it for survival.

- **What is the most significant activity that rangers like George do?**

NEWS DETECTIVE   by Emily Sohn

The 20-mile [32-km] hike to the top of Mount Holmes and back had its ups and downs, both physically and emotionally. It was freezing cold when we got up at 4:30 that morning. At the start of the hike, I was wearing a wool hat, long pants, and all my layers of fleece and polypro. My fingers were numb from the chill. By mid-morning, the sun was blazing hot and the mosquitoes were biting. As we gained in altitude, the temperature dropped again and breathing grew more difficult.

A mile or two from the top, the trail dead-ended right into this glacier field. We searched around and around. Finally, we just walked up the steep ridge, one slow step at a time, hoping we were going in the right direction. Eventually, we did bump into the rocky trail again, which took us to the summit and George Henley.

YELLOWSTONE WONDERS

Ever since Yellowstone became the first U.S. national park in 1872, it has been a prime tourist destination. It's easy to see why. Old Faithful and other geysers spout water high into the air. Pungent gases bubble up through mud. Rivers of scalding hot water carve beautiful, alien landscapes that stink of sulfur.

Then, there are the animals. As we drove and hiked through the park, my friend Gabe and I felt like we were

The hike back down was more straightforward. We knew where we were going, and we had fun talking about George most of the way. After 10 hours of hiking, though, our bodies were exhausted. We ran out of water. My feet were killing me. With about 1 mile to go, we ran right into a pack of wild bison. Neither of us wanted to walk any farther than we had to, so we held our breaths and tiptoed right past the massive creatures. I tried not to make eye contact, especially with the Mama bison who was guarding her baby.

Twenty minutes later, we were safely back in the parking lot. I have never been so happy to see a car in my entire life. We drove straight to some natural hot springs at the north end of the park. As the hot water soothed our weary muscles, and later over an enormous dinner, we reflected on what a great day it had been. Then, we went back to camp and slept for a long, long time.

on a safari. We saw grizzly bears, elk, bison, wolves, antelope, and more.

We weren't the only ones impressed by Yellowstone's **geology** and wildlife. An 11-year-old girl named Tessa, whose family was visiting the park from Seattle, was so impressed by the steaming hot-spring pools that she was writing down their names in a notebook.

"Lots of minerals!" Tessa said, when I asked her what part of the park was her favorite. Her 10-year-old brother Wesley looked bored until he started listing the animals he had seen so far—black bears, elk, deer, grasshoppers, prairie dogs—and the animals he still hoped to see: moose, wolves, jackrabbits.

- **Can you name three reasons that Yellowstone National Park is a popular tourist spot?**

WILDFIRES LARGE AND SMALL

Fires deserve just as much attention as rocks and bears, Renkin insists. "We see the effects of fire on the landscape everywhere we look," he says. "Even when you are looking at trees that are green, they are all born from an earlier fire."

Most fires are small, Renkin says. They usually burn themselves out before they cause too much damage. And even though 3 years out of every 10 are dry enough to be serious fire years, historical records show that really big

Figure 1.3 Wildfires happen frequently in places that are prone to drought, like Yellowstone National Park.

fires strike the Yellowstone area only once every 200 to 400 years.

"We don't get them very frequently," Renkin says. "But when we do get them, we get them very, very hot, and we get total stand replacement."

The summer of 1988 was a perfect example. That year, not a single drop of rain fell in August in the northern part of the park. "In 106 years of the fire record, we don't see that anywhere," Renkin says. "That was really something."

At the same time, the park was full of big trees, some more than 200 years old. Renkin's research has shown that old trees burn faster than young ones.

Together, those conditions were a recipe for disaster. More than 45 fires swept through Yellowstone that summer, Renkin says. Lightning ignited most of them. People started others. Fires burned for longer than 3 months and consumed more than 34,000 acres [13,759 hectares] of forest until late summer rains and snow finally put them out. "The sheer magnitude of these fires was so awesome," Renkin says. "There were miles and miles of fire front moving along."

- **Why were there so many fires in Yellowstone in the summer of 1988? What are some of the major causes of forest fires?**

FIRE'S BENEFITS

Even today, 15 years later, charred logs and dead trunks litter the park. On our hike to Mount Holmes, Gabe and I passed through barren stands of blackened timber instead of lush blankets of trees that used to cover the base of the mountain. It saddened us that so many trees and animals had died in the blaze.

On a long time scale, however, the 1988 fires started a whole slew of important events. Big fires clear the way for what scientists call succession. Winds blow in new seeds that take root in the bare soil. Because heat rises, bulbs and other underground plant parts often survive and sprout again.

It takes fallen logs 70 to 100 years to decompose, Renkin says. During that time, nutrients seep back into the dirt to feed future generations of plants and animals.

Some plants even rely on fire to reproduce. Lodgepole pines, the most common tree in Yellowstone, have a type of pinecone that sits in the treetops for years. In order to open and release their seeds, the cones need heat from a fire to unseal the glue-like resin that keeps them shut.

For all of these reasons, rangers at Yellowstone usually leave fire alone. "It kind of takes the forest back to a starting point," Renkin says, "and the whole process starts all over again."

- When scientist talk about succession, what are they referring to? How do big fires contribute to succession?

- What reasons do rangers give for letting some fires burn in Yellowstone?

LIFE ON A MOUNTAINTOP

No one is in a better position to observe this cycle of life and death than George Henley.

Over the years, he has watched the decline of black bears in the park, for one thing. Bears used to be so common, he told us, that a mama bear and her two cubs once broke into his house, when he lived in a different part of the park. George later found them sitting in the woods, eating his can of cocoa.

There are also unexpected sightings. He once alerted park rangers when a rare group of mountain goats appeared near his lookout.

George has become an expert at spotting fires and reading weather. After we had finished eating lunch in his hut, he showed us his equipment: thermometers to measure temperature and dew point, wooden sticks that he weighs to calculate moisture in the air, a weather vane to read wind direction, and more. He calls all his readings in to park headquarters at about 1:30 P.M. every day.

I was most impressed by the Osborne Firefinder—an ancient-looking contraption that spins around and allows him to pinpoint the location of a fire on a map. The day we arrived, the viewfinder was pointed at a small blaze way down in a valley to the southwest. It had been burning for two days. "It's picking up pretty good," George noted.

To pass the many hours he spends alone, George reads books, works on his ham radio, and keeps a journal. Daily journal entries cover the things that you notice when you live on a mountaintop: animals, weather, fires. On Friday, August 21, 2001, for example, George wrote: "It was pleasant and sunny today, so I washed clothes."

If only life could always be so simple.

After Reading:

- **Roy Renkin, the vegetation management specialist, has determined through research that old trees burn faster than young ones. Can you think of any reasons why this is true?**

- **How can sticks help measure humidity? Would a lighter or heavier stick indicate a higher level of humidity?**

- **Why does George Henley have to keep records of the wind and temperature in the park? What conditions would cause the strongest wildfires?**

Conserving Energy at Home

You've probably heard your parents tell you to turn down the heat or air conditioning to "save energy." Just how much energy does it take to keep your home cool in summer and warm in winter? And what steps can you take to use the energy available responsibly? In the following article, writer Emily Sohn looks at the issue of climate control and the concept of "green" houses—homes that make the best possible use of energy in order to help protect the environment.

—The Editor

Cold House, Hot House, Green House

by Emily Sohn

Before Reading:

- **Name three things that you use or do that waste energy.**

- **What do you think "sustainable" means? What might "sustainable architecture" involve?**

When it's cold outside, you turn on the heat. When it's hot, you turn on the air conditioning. That's about as much thought as most people ever give to temperature control at home.

You might want to dwell a little longer on the conditioned air that magically wafts out of household vents, however. The way you heat or cool your home has a big effect on the Earth, says John Carmody. He's director of the Center for Sustainable Building Research at the University of Minnesota in Minneapolis.

"Most people don't usually think about where their heat comes from," Carmody says. Yet nearly every type of energy source dumps waste or spews pollution into the air.

Buildings have a huge impact on the environment. There are more than 81 million buildings in the United

States, according to the U.S. Department of Energy. Buildings consume more energy than any other economic category, including transportation and industry. Almost half of the energy that buildings use goes into heating and cooling.

Like Carmody, a growing number of engineers, planners, and architects have been looking for new ways to make buildings less wasteful and kinder to the environment. Improvements have come in many forms, including better insulation, windows, and construction materials.

- How does the energy used in the United States for heating and cooling affect the environment?

Architects are also realizing that the size, location, and positioning of a building affects how much energy it uses. Even the arrangement of buildings in a neighborhood makes a difference.

"In the last 10 years," Carmody says, "there has been a major movement toward what you'd call '**green**' buildings." Such buildings are sometimes also described as sustainable, environmentally friendly, or healthy.

TEMPERATURE CONTROL

- Define the term "green building" in your own words.

The amount of energy you use for heating and cooling depends on where you live.

In places such as San Diego, California, for instance, the temperature is mild all year round. People rarely have to regulate the temperature of their homes.

Where I live in Minnesota, on the other hand, winters are unbearably cold, and summers can be unbearably hot. Without heaters and air conditioners, we'd be in big trouble. (At least, I know I would be pretty miserable.)

To get a sense of your own environmental impact, you can look at the climate where you live. Ask yourself how often you turn on the heater or the air conditioner, and how high you pump them up.

You might also want to figure out the source of the energy that your house or school uses for temperature control. Most air conditioners run on electricity. Some heaters do, too. If you find a furnace in the basement and radiators around your house, though, that probably means you have a system that burns natural gas or oil to heat water.

These energy sources have their down sides. Electricity, for example, usually comes from power plants that burn coal or use nuclear fuel. Both produce dangerous waste.

And there's energy lost along the way. "Only about a third of the energy generated at a power plant makes its way to a house," Carmody says.

As an alternative energy source,

> • **In what ways might the generation of electricity at power plants be bad for the environment?**

harnessing the power of the wind or sun is becoming more popular in some places. Windmills for generating electricity are springing up from California to Germany. And researchers are working to make **solar cells**, which absorb light from the sun and convert it into electricity, more efficient.

Sunlight can also be used to heat tanks of water. Still, the technology needs some work. For now, solar power is more expensive than traditional sources. And some places don't have enough reliable sunshine or wind to make these approaches practical.

WINDOWS, WALLS, AND ROOFS

No matter where the energy comes from to heat or cool your home, simple design and construction choices can have a big effect on how much energy you end up using.

First, consider when your home was built. Old houses tend to be drafty, Carmody says. They lose energy to the outdoors.

Newer buildings have more insulation packed into the walls. Fluffy materials such as fiberglass and Styrofoam® have lots of pockets for trapping air. Such a structure holds heat in, just like a cozy sleeping bag. Many environmentalists prefer cellulose fiber, which is made from recycled paper and wood, for insulation.

When it comes to energy efficiency, windows are a

big issue. Instead of just looking through them, take a closer look at the windows where you live. If you can feel cold air rushing in even when the window is closed, that's a good sign that you're wasting a lot of energy.

New technologies are drastically improving window performance.

Windows used to be made from single sheets of glass. Today, windows are almost always double-glazed. This means there are two panes of glass set in a frame with an air space between them for insulation. Sometimes, windows are triple-glazed.

Scientists have also developed special coatings for windows. These invisible materials reflect heat. In a double-glazed window, coating the two sides of glass that face each other traps heat between the panes and increases insulation.

Chemists in England recently developed a kind of "smart" window coating. It reflects heat, but only when the window gets warmer than room temperature. If the technology becomes more affordable and practical, it could make windows even better at keeping the inside air in and the outside air out.

On the other side of the temperature fence, researchers from Oak Ridge and Lawrence Berkeley National Laboratories are working

- **How have windows changed and improved over the years?**

on a new type of roofing material that they hope will cut the cost of air conditioning by 20%.

If you've ever worn a black T-shirt on a sunny day, you know that dark colors absorb light and create heat. Most roofs are dark, so they absorb **infrared** and visible light, which makes a building warmer. The idea is to make shingles with colors that reflect certain wavelengths of sunlight. Such "cool" roofs should be available in three to five years, the scientists say.

• **How can roofing materials help make homes more energy efficient?**

LIVING SPACES

Perhaps the most innovative strategy for increasing energy efficiency actually has nothing to do with technology. Instead, architects take advantage of the environment and landscape to control temperature inside a building.

In the Northern Hemisphere, this can mean installing lots of south-facing windows so that plenty of sunlight can pour in. At the same time, well-designed overhangs keep summer sun out but let winter sun in.

Some people are choosing to live in communities that have been specifically designed to promote energy-efficient living. Village Homes in Davis, California, was one of the first of such green, or sustainable, developments.

Completed in 1981, the neighborhood has a network

of paths that encourages people to bike or walk instead of drive (and pollute). The development's 240 houses face south for lots of exposure to the sun. Overhangs provide shade. Houses run on solar power. There are lots of trees. And narrow streets have as little pavement as possible.

The strategy seems to be working. The air temperature around Village Homes is 15 degrees F [-9.4°C] cooler than surrounding areas that have more pavement. And residents spend between one-third and one-half as much on energy bills compared to more conventional homes in nearby neighborhoods.

"We have a shadier, cooler microclimate," says developer and resident Judith Corbett, who spoke at an environmental design conference in Minneapolis in April 2004. "I don't even have an air conditioner."

As people see communities such as Village Homes thrive, these types of developments are becoming more popular. They're springing up in places such as Colorado, Arizona, Virginia, and Australia.

ZERO ENERGY

The U.S. government itself is taking steps to boost the energy efficiency of the nation's buildings. In one project, the Department of Energy has a long-term goal to create a "net-zero-energy" house—a house that wastes no energy.

The Department of Energy's development of "near-zero-energy" homes is one step in that direction. One such house in Tennessee runs completely on electricity for just 82 cents a day. Conventional homes in the same area use between $4 and $5 in electricity a day.

• **What is a "net-zero-energy" house?**

As research on efficient energy use continues, think about what you can do to live a more energy-efficient life in the meantime.

Keep the heat low or off when you're not home. Make sure leaks around doors and windows get patched. Turn off lights, TVs, and computers when they're not needed.

Better yet, if you're cold, put on a sweater and have a hot drink. If you're hot, consider having an ice cream cone or going for a swim.

After Reading:

• Do an energy survey of your home. For a form you can fill out, go to *www.eia.doe.gov/kids/classactivities/HomeSurveyPrimary.pdf*. Look for places where energy might be going to waste. For additional information about what to look for in your home, see *www.ase.org/uploaded_files/educatorlessonplans/audit.pdf*. What recommendations would you have for improving the energy efficiency of your home?

- Pick a building that you often go into. It can be your school or home, a friend's house, a local library, or some other building. How would you test this building's energy efficiency? What sort of data would you collect?

- Why do you think more buildings don't get updated to be made "greener"?

- What are the energy or environmental concerns in the area where you live? Design a house that you think might best serve the region in which you live.

- Although lots of technologies exist to make homes more environmentally friendly, the U.S. government and local governments generally don't require such improvements. Why do you think there are very few such requirements? How would life be different if the government did require people to update their homes to improve energy efficiency?

- Besides changing the architecture or materials of a home, what are some other ways to have a household use less energy?

Section 2

Climate Change

The Earth's climate is always changing. Over many millions of years, the Earth has warmed and cooled more times than scientists have yet been able to count. But today, climate seems to be changing at an unprecedented rate. In part because of pollution and the chemicals humans have let out into the atmosphere, the Earth has begun to get warmer and warmer. Although the changes are not always noticeable to us, many other species of animals are definitely noticing—and some of them are dying. In this section, we look at the issue of climate change, and the steps environmentalists are taking to try to stop the rapid warming of the globe.

In the first article, author Emily Sohn describes the ways climate changes occur and points out methods scientists use to keep track of changing climate patterns. The second article highlights the role of the algae that live in arctic regions in helping environmentalist figure out how quickly the Earth is warming up. Finally, we look at the ways climate change affects certain species—in particular, monarch butterflies, whose migration habits are closely linked to the climate in which they live.

—The Editor

Global Warming

Over the last century, the average temperature on Earth has risen by about 33°F (0.6°C). At first glance, this may not seem like a huge change, but it has dramatically affected plants and animals, if not humans. Living things that make their homes in cool, wet places have trouble surviving as the weather gets warmer and drier. If it continues at its current place, global warming could kill off many species of fish and other creatures. In the following article, author Emily Sohn describes what global warming is, how it affects living things, and what might be done to help stop it.

—The Editor

A Change in Climate

by Emily Sohn

Before Reading:

- **What might cause global warming?**

- **Why are changes in climate reason for concern?**

From one day to the next, weather can have a big effect on your life. When it rains, you have to stay indoors or carry an umbrella. When it's cold, you have to bundle up.

Over the course of hundreds, thousands, and millions of years, weather trends affect life on Earth in more dramatic ways. Ice ages or long droughts, for example, can wipe out certain types of plants and animals. Although many species manage to survive such extreme, long-term climate shifts, their living conditions also change.

There's lots of evidence of drastic changes in climate occurring in the distant past. Earth today may again be in the midst of such a climate change. In the last 100 years, studies show, global temperatures have risen an average of 0.6 degrees C [33.1°F].

That might not sound so bad. After all, what difference does half a degree make?

A growing number of studies suggest, however, that such an increase could have a big impact on life.

Biologists and ecologists are discovering, often by accident, that climate change is forcing some plants and animals into new **habitats**. Others are becoming extinct. Sometimes, scientists show up at a site they've studied for years, only to discover that the organisms they've been tracking are no longer there. What's more, it now looks like this redistribution of life on Earth is sometimes happening at an alarmingly fast pace.

"These little pieces of information are all warning signs that stuff is going on," says Erik Beever. He's a research ecologist with the United States Geological Survey in Corvallis, Oregon. "Our world is changing more rapidly than we have observed in the recent past," he says.

TREE LINE

One place to look for changes in plant and animal life that may be caused by a climate shift is in the mountains.

As the globe warms up, mountaintops get warmer, too. Trees start growing at higher altitudes than before. The tree line shifts upward.

In the Alps, a mountain range in Europe, records from the last 80 to 100 years show that plants have been working their way upward at a rate of about 4 meters [13 feet] every decade. Researchers from the University of Vienna found this trend in two-thirds of the sites they checked.

In one recent study in Nevada, Beever discovered that a type of tree called the Engleman spruce had moved its habitat upslope a dramatic 650 feet [198 meters] in just 9 years. "The site at the lowest elevation went from 41 individuals to just 6," he says. At higher elevations, numbers increased.

- **How can even slight changes in average temperature affect plants and animals and their habitats?**

- **"Our world is changing more rapidly than we have observed in the recent past," Erik Beever says. Why does he say this? Where do scientists notice this shift?**

"When I first saw the results," Beever says, "I had a really hard time believing it because it's just too fast."

Beever's analysis of the data suggests that global warming is mainly responsible for the shift. Studies in mountain ranges from New Zealand to Spain reveal similar trends.

GLOBAL WARMING

What's causing today's increased temperatures?

Many scientists say that human activities, such as burning coal, oil, and other **fossil fuels**, are largely to blame. These activities release heat-trapping gases, such as carbon dioxide, into the atmosphere. The more these gases accumulate in the atmosphere, the hotter things get on Earth.

Some experts remain skeptical. They point out that natural causes may be playing an important role in today's global temperature increases. The same factors that caused ice ages, extreme heat waves, and massive droughts in the past before human activities were important could still be at work now.

In the case of rising tree lines, they say, trees may still be recovering from an unusually cool period, known as the Little Ice Age, which lasted from the 1300s into the middle of the 1800s. It's even possible that efforts to put out fires allow plants to move into new habitats.

• **When was the Little Ice Age?**

MOUNTAIN ISLANDS

Scientists predict that average temperatures may go up another 1.4 to 5.8 degrees [34.5 to 42.4°F] in the next 100 years. If it occurs, such a rapid increase wouldn't give plants and animals much time to adapt to new conditions.

Organisms that live on mountains may face the grimmest future. That's because mountaintops are, in many ways, like islands. They're isolated clearings that poke up above the tree line.

Although it's too cold for trees to grow at such heights, these alpine environments are ideal habitats for some animals, which have become highly specialized to live there.

"A lot of populations are just little frostings on peaks," says James Brown. Brown is a population ecologist at the University of New Mexico, who was recently quoted in the journal *Science*.

Like animals on islands, these mountaintop creatures have no escape if conditions change.

PICK A PIKA

One of the most direct and dramatic demonstrations of the impact of **global warming**, Beever says, comes from a furry little creature called the pika.

- **Why are mountaintops more vulnerable to climate change than other habitats?**

Hands down, pikas are among the most adorable animals you'll ever see in the wild. Though related to rabbits, they look like furry little gerbils. "Even as a male, I can say they're cute," Beever says. "They're pretty nifty little guys."

To see pikas, you have to go high up on a mountain because they can't survive warm weather. In a famous study in the 1970s, a scientist put pikas in cages at low elevations to see what would happen. Many of the animals died, even in the shade. It was just too hot for them.

Their habits make pikas particularly vulnerable to increased temperatures. "They don't move a lot," Beever says. "A one-mile migration for a pika would be a huge, huge, huge deal, and a pretty rare event, as far as we know." In other words, when conditions change, pikas can't do much about it.

For more than 10 years, Beever has been surveying pika populations in the mountain states of the U.S. West. By the end of 1999, he had confirmed that 7 out of 25 populations that he had originally surveyed were gone. More recently, Beever found that two more populations have disappeared.

• In what ways has the pika population changed in the last 10 years? Why?

EARLY WARNING

Not all species are threatened by rising temperatures. Some plants and animals like it hot and dry. Others can move or adapt to get the cold or moisture they need to survive.

Pikas are different. "Pikas are an early warning sign," Beever. "They are very clearly vulnerable to high temperatures."

So, the case of the disappearing pikas is reason enough to wake up and take notice, he says. Something in the weather is changing, and the trends look alarming.

But, Beever says, there are things that you can do that

may help. Choices you make every day—such as walking instead of going in a car—can add up. By reducing the levels of carbon dioxide and other **greenhouse gases** in the air, we may be able to slow the warming trend.

> • **What are some of the things you can do to help prevent global warming?**

If nothing else, do it for the pikas. The world could always use a little extra cuteness.

After Reading:

- How would you look for evidence of climate change in the area in which you live? What might be some indicators of changes in climate? What sort of data could you collect?

- Why is the speed of the change in average temperature especially worrisome to scientists?

- Besides mountaintops, what other areas might be especially vulnerable to climate change?

- If Earth were getting colder rather than warmer, what dangers might there be for animals and plants in various habitats?

- In addition to the suggestions made in the article, what other simple things could you do to change your daily life to help prevent global warming?

Algae as Early Warning Devices

Although scientists often disagree about how severe the problem of global warming is, there is little doubt that climate change does affect certain species of living things— especially those that live in the water. Aquatic animals and plants are very sensitive to even slight changes in temperature. As their environment heats up, they may have trouble staying alive. In the next article, writer Emily Sohn shows how the algae that live in arctic areas are helping scientists study the effects of global warming.

—The Editor

Arctic Algae Show Climate Change

by Emily Sohn

Tiny creatures in remote lakes are adding to the evidence for global warming. Most scientists agree that the climate is heating up. Studies of environments all over the world show that the warming has wide-ranging effects.

A recent study focused on changes at high altitudes way up north from Canada to Russia. Many of the lakes were on islands in the Arctic Ocean. They were too far away from civilization for people's activities to directly influence them.

These lakes freeze over in the winter. That makes the plants and animals that live in them very sensitive to changes in climate. If temperatures warm up even just a few degrees, algae have a longer growing season and so do the animals that eat the plant material.

To learn more about how aquatic life has changed over the years in these remote places, scientists from Queen's University in Kingston, Ontario, took 55 samples of sediment from the bottoms of dozens of lakes.

Within the samples, they counted remains of tiny creatures including water fleas, insect **larvae**, and algae called **diatoms**. The team recorded the numbers of these

53

lake inhabitants at different depths. The deeper the sediment, the older it is.

Results showed that ecosystems started to change in many of the lakes about 150 years ago. Populations of water fleas and algae-eating insect larvae increased, for example. And one type of diatom replaced another.

The researchers speculate that the shift was a result of climate change. Warming kept lakes unfrozen for a longer period each year, they say. Some species thrive in those conditions. Others do worse.

The new study didn't look at what is causing global warming in the first place. Instead, it illustrates that minor shifts in temperature can have major effects on life around the globe.

Going Deeper:

Perkins, Sid. "Warm Spell: Arctic Algae Record Shift in Climate." *Science News* 167 (March 5, 2005): 148. Available online at *http://www.sciencenews.org/articles/20050305/fob3.asp*.

Migrating Monarchs and Global Warming

You may have seen pictures of beautiful monarch butter-flies flying in massive swarms as they migrate to warmer climates when the weather starts to get cold. Millions of these creatures move every winter from their homes in the United States and Canada to Mexico, where the warm weather helps them survive the change of seasons. As the threat of global warming continues to increase, scientists are beginning to worry about the fate of the monarchs. If climate changes bring increased precipitation in warm places like Mexico, as environmentalists believe may happen, the monarchs might not be able to go there to spend the winter and survive.

—The Editor

Will Climate Change Depose Monarchs?

by Emily Sohn

If you've ever seen a flock of migrating monarch butterflies, you're one of the lucky ones. Fifty years from now, your memory might be all that's left of the flapping beauties (Figure 2.1).

A computer analysis suggests that some populations of monarch butterflies could die out in North America if the weather in Mexico changes.

Monarch butterflies fly great distances to spend their winters in warm places. Butterflies that spend their summers in the western United States and Canada migrate to beaches in California during the winter. Monarchs that live east of the Rockies bask in the Mexican sun all winter long. Some 200 million butterflies make the trip every year.

Karen Oberhauser of the University of Minnesota at Minneapolis, St. Paul and a colleague used a computer model to predict the future of January weather in the dozen or so places in Mexico where the butterflies usually go.

The computer analysis predicted that temperatures in the butterflies' Mexican habitats would stay monarch-

Figure 2.1 Migrating monarch butterflies are an incredible sight to behold as they make their way from the United States and Canada to Mexico and other warmer locations.

friendly. Precipitation, on the other hand, would more than triple by 2050. Monarch butterflies have never been known to survive in such wet conditions.

If the climate in Mexico changes as predicted, researchers hope that the butterflies will adapt by finding other places to spend their winters. The research also shows just how challenging and uncertain life can be for animals that migrate long distances every year.

Going Deeper:

Milius, Susan. "Will Climate Change Depose Monarchs? Model Predicts Too-wet Winter Refuges." *Science News* 164 (November 15, 2003): 310. Available online at *http://www.sciencenews.org/20031115/fob7.asp*.

You can learn more about monarch butterfly migrations online at *www.learner.org/jnorth/fall2003/monarch/index.html*.

Section 3

Wildlife Protection

Species go extinct all the time—it's the nature of life. But today, as human beings clear land to make room for homes and factories, and spew pollution into the air and the sea, many more plants and animals are dying than normal. Environmentalists have recognized how critical it is to protect those animals that are declining in number, and to find ways to keep them from going prematurely extinct. In this section, we explore the issue of wildlife protection, with a look at some of the particular animals that are in danger and the programs being put in place to help save them.

In the first article, author Kate Ramsayer examines the plight of the spotted owl. As the numbers of these endangered birds continue to decline, controversy has arisen over how the owls can be protected without ruining economic opportunities for the humans who use the trees and other resources that are part of the owls' habitat.

If you've ever been lucky enough to see a fierce tiger or elephant at a zoo or circus, you know the wild majesty of these creatures. In the second and third articles, writer Emily Sohn takes a look at how tigers and elephants are disappearing from their native homes because of hunting, human encroachment, and other problems, and the steps scientists and government officials are taking to try to keep them alive.

—The Editor

Saving the Spotted Owl

The spotted owl of the Pacific Northwest has become one of the most controversial protected animals in the recent history of the environmental movement. Because their habitat is a prime location for choice timber, many industrialists risk financial setback in their business if they are not permitted to cut down trees when the government extends protection to owls. At the same time, the spotted owl has been put in danger by something besides human activity—other owls invading their home territory. In the following article, author Kate Ramsayer explains the threats to the spotted owl and what the owls' declining numbers mean for the environment.

—The Editor

Spotty Survival

by Kate Ramsayer

Before Reading:

- **Name an endangered or threatened species in the area where you live. Is anything being done to help save this species? See** *http://endangered.fws.gov/* **(U.S. Fish and Wildlife Service).**

- **Why might it be important to save a species from extinction?**

Biologist Lowell Diller knows how to make friends with a northern spotted owl.

He gently strokes the feathers on the bird's forehead, right above its eyes. The owl, which had been flapping around as Diller held its feet, immediately calms down. It gazes up at Diller, almost in a trance, as the biologist measures its size and weight, makes sure it's healthy, and slips an identification tag around its foot.

He wants to make the owl feel as relaxed as possible. That way, if he needs to catch it again, the bird might remember the head massage and the free mice Diller feeds it and not immediately fly away.

Diller keeps track of spotted owls as part of his job.

NEWS DETECTIVE   by Kate Ramsayer

I was standing with a group of journalists in a forest, listening to Lowell Diller talk about dusky-footed woodrats, when something caught a reporter's eye.

Isn't that a spotted owl, he asked, pointing up to a tree branch. Sure enough, gazing down at us with huge dark eyes, there sat a northern spotted owl. We quickly lost interest in the woodrats, the preferred meal of northern California spotted owls, and gathered around where the owl was perched.

We soon spied three more owls—another adult and two very fuzzy juveniles. The adult male was new to the area, so Diller wanted to tag it. Our group, on a fellowship program with the Institutes for Journalism and Natural Resources (*www.ijnr.org/*), was more than willing to watch and help out.

To lure the owl, Diller had a reporter jiggle a cat toy on the end of a string, just enough to distract the owl. Then he came in from the side and slipped a leash around the owl's neck. It's a tricky business, he said, because you don't want the owl flying off and hurting itself.

Diller skillfully pulled the owl to him and held it tight, grasping its feet in one hand and stroking its forehead with the other. The owl appeared to love that and relaxed completely. Any time it got antsy, all Diller had to do was stroke

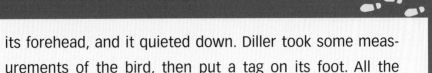

its forehead, and it quieted down. Diller took some measurements of the bird, then put a tag on its foot. All the while, the three other birds watched with interest.

To make sure the owls were left with a good opinion of people, Diller also gave them a little treat. He had brought along a box of unsuspecting white mice, which we held up, one at a time, on a big stick.

The adult owls swooped in silently to grab the squeaking mice. They ate some of the mice and brought others back to their fuzzy offspring.

During the fellowship, we got to do some pretty amazing things, such as canoeing, hiking through redwood forests, searching for salamanders in a stream, visiting the site of the Biscuit Fire that burned half a million acres, taking a smelly tour of a fish-processing factory, and talking to all sorts of people with all kinds of opinions.

But getting to see the spotted owls up close was a high point for me. I was awed by the sight of these birds and amazed at how much they seemed to trust people. I hope they'll be around for people to admire for a long time to come.

- **How does biologist Lowell Diller get a spotted owl to relax? Why does he do this?**

He's a senior biologist at Green Diamond Resource Company, a timber company based in Seattle. Ever since 1990, when the United States government declared northern spotted owls a threatened species, timber companies must make sure they don't harm or disturb the birds.

On government lands, big chunks of owl-friendly habitat are set aside, off-limits to loggers.

But northern spotted owls are still in trouble. The number of owls is declining in many areas, and they face threats that won't easily disappear. For example, the barred owl appears to be bullying spotted owls out of their territories. And some scientists are concerned that spotted owls might start dying from **West Nile virus**.

"Right now there's more uncertainty than there has been, in my opinion, and it's because of these two unknown threats," Diller says. "We can't predict how they're going to turn out."

- **What are the main threats to the survival of northern spotted owl?**

DECLINING NUMBERS

Northern spotted owls live in the western parts of northern California, Oregon, Washington, and British Columbia. They roost in stands of trees that are hundreds of years old.

In these old-growth forests, large trees mix with smaller trees, with dead trees called snags, and with trees having broken tops or holes in which the owls can make their nests. Some studies suggest that the owls can also live in forests made up of younger trees, as long as there's still a variety of sizes and types of trees.

But, as settlers moved into the Pacific Northwest, many cut down vast numbers of trees for timber. One study estimates that, since the early 1800s, people destroyed between 60% and 88% of potential spotted owl habitat.

> • **Where do northern spotted owls live? In what sorts of places do they like to nest?**

The loss was so great that, when forest managers started protecting owl habitat 14 years ago, they suspected that the number of spotted owls wouldn't immediately bounce back. Now, the number of owls in northern California and parts of Oregon is holding steady, but the owl population in Washington and British Columbia is getting smaller.

"Some of the populations are still continuing to decline," says Rocky Gutierrez. He studies spotted owls as a professor at the University of Minnesota. "But others have shown a stabilizing trend," he says. "We think that's due to the protection of habitat."

BULLYING BIRDS?

Scientists have a possible suspect for the decline.

"In the past 60 years or so, the barred owl has invaded the range of the northern spotted owl," Gutierrez says. "The stage is set for competition to occur."

And, so far, it looks like the barred owl is winning. Previously, barred owls lived in the eastern United States. Slowly but surely, they migrated across Canada and down the West Coast, into spotted owl territory.

Barred owls are closely related to northern spotted owls, but they are slightly bigger. They live in the same habitats as spotted owls do and eat similar food, although they seem less finicky.

- **Why are barred owls a threat to the spotted owl? Where did they come from?**

Barred owls are also more aggressive. Some scientists say that the barred owls are kicking spotted owls out of the few areas where spotted owls can live.

"The biggest wild card right now is the barred owl," says Robin Bown. She's a biologist with the U.S. Fish and Wildlife Service. "If you create the habitat, you don't know if you're going to get barred owls or spotted owls."

Still, scientists can't be sure that the barred owls are causing the decline in spotted owls. Right now, they only have observations, Bown says. They can see that there are fewer spotted owls in areas where there are more barred owls, but they don't have any direct proof that barred owls are the culprit.

Gutierrez is interested in doing experiments to test the idea scientifically. He is planning to play recordings of barred owl calls and spotted owl calls near sites where spotted owls nest. He'll play different combinations of the recordings to see if the spotted owls respond after the barred owl calls or if they keep quiet, not wanting to attract attention.

"At this point there's a great deal of scientific uncertainty about how these two species interact," he says.

- **How is Gutierrez trying to determine whether the barred owl is negatively affecting the spotted owl?**

But if barred owls turn out to be the bullies of old-growth forests, people can't simply make rules to make them share the forest, as they did to slow down logging.

"The biggest problem is that there's not much you can do," Bown says. Instead, biologists can only hope that the two species of owls learn to live together. Or, perhaps spotted owls will settle into a habitat that their barred owl cousins don't like. It's an issue that scientists will keep a close eye on.

OTHER THREATS

Spotted owl biologists are also paying attention to other

threats. Recently, West Nile virus has infected several birds of prey. While there haven't been any known cases of West Nile among spotted owls, Diller says it could happen this spring.

Certain species of birds are resistant to West Nile and don't get sick. But some birds die when infected. The biologists will just have to wait and see what happens with spotted owls.

Weather can also play a role in spotted owl survival. Rain ruffles the owls' feathers so that they can't fly as quietly to sneak up on their prey. If the spring is wet and owls can't catch as many flying squirrels or dusky-footed woodrats, they might not have any chicks.

- **In what ways does rain affect the northern spotted owl?**

Although there are many factors that people can't control, there are some factors they can control.

"Habitat is still an issue, and, if anything, it may be a bigger issue now because we're losing spotted owl sites to barred owls," Bown says.

So, forest managers are continuing to set aside patches of federal land for owls. On timber company lands, biologists such as Diller are drawing up habitat conservation plans to make up for areas the companies log.

Still, it looks like spotted owls will need help from all the friends they can get.

After Reading:

- Why might scientists be interested in saving the northern spotted owl?

- How might efforts to save the spotted owl be similar to attempts to save other endangered species and how might they be different?

- The deaths of birds often serve as a signal that the West Nile virus is present in an area. Why does the disease show up so quickly in certain birds? For additional information about West Nile virus and birds, see *www.nwhc.usgs.gov/ research/west_nile/west_nile.html* (*U.S. Geological Survey*) and *www.audubon.org/ bird/wnv/* (*National Audubon Society*).

- Are animals that are predators more likely to go extinct than other animals? Why or why not?

- Come up with two questions that you might want to ask of a biologist who studies spotted owls.

- Given the different threats that spotted owls face, how much control do scientists have in trying to save the birds? If you had some money to give toward an effort to save the owls, how should the money be used? Why?

- What might account for the observation that the population of spotted owls is declining in British Columbia and Washington but staying steady in Oregon and California?

Taking Care of India's Tigers

Living in North America, most of us don't get a chance to see tigers on a regular basis—and even when we do, it's most likely as part of an exhibit in a zoo, not in the wild that is the great cats' home. In India, seeing a tiger is a slightly more common occurrence—but that may be changing. As author Emily Sohn explains in the next article, tigers are slowly dying out in India, even with vast wildlife preserves set aside for them. The Indian people are taking dramatic steps in an attempt to protect the tiger—an ancient symbol that is a powerful part of their heritage.

—The Editor

Missing Tigers in India

by Emily Sohn

Before Reading:

- **Have you ever seen a tiger (not including a photo of one)? If so, where?**

- **What wild animals do you imagine live in India?**

Ranthambore National Park, India. I knew they were out there somewhere, and I was determined to find them.

Like most tourists who visit Ranthambore National Park in India, I went with just one goal in mind: to see tigers in the wild.

Twice a day, all year round, 10 open-topped trucks are allowed to rumble along the park's dirt roads for a few hours. It costs 360 rupees (about $8, U.S.) to buy a seat on one of the trucks. Glimpses of tigers are free.

Of course, nothing is guaranteed. Forty tigers roam Ranthambore's 388 square miles [1,005 km^2]. But tigers hear and smell us long before we can see them. Some tourists I met near the park were lucky enough to see a handful of tigers up close during just one safari. Other people saw none, even after going out six or more times.

Still, I couldn't pass up the excursion. It was an opportunity that might someday disappear. Tigers are among the most endangered animals on Earth.

In India, where about half of the planet's remaining 7,000 wild tigers live, tigers face a number of threats, especially from a growing human population. More than a billion people live in India today, and development is rapidly expanding into what was once largely tiger territory.

Conservationists nonetheless remain optimistic. "The tiger will not disappear," said P. K. Sen, director of the Tiger and Wildlife Program for World Wildlife Fund–India (WWF–India). He was kind enough to meet with me in his New Delhi office on a Sunday, the only day I spent in the city during a recent three-week trip to India.

There's no way, Sen said, that people will ever let the majestic cats die out. "The tiger has been a symbol of strength and might for thousands of years," he said.

MAJESTIC CATS

Hundreds of years ago, there were many more tigers on Earth than there are today. An estimated 40,000 tigers used to live in India, Sen said, an area that once included modern-day Pakistan, Bangladesh, and other neighboring lands.

From the beginning, tigers inspired awe, respect, and fear in people. And with good reason. An adult male

Bengal tiger may weigh more than 500 pounds [227 kg].

The graceful cats stalk, crouch, and explosively pounce on their prey, which includes deer, pigs, cattle, and other large animals. To kill, they grab the prey by its neck and either snap its spinal cord or suffocate the animal. One tiger can eat more than 40 pounds [18 kg] of fresh meat in one sitting.

Tigers repeatedly star in Indian stories as symbols of power and strength. The powerful Hindu god Shiva, for one, is often shown wearing a tiger skin. The Hindu goddess Durga rides a tiger into battle, symbolizing her ability to defeat demons that no one else can vanquish.

- **Describe the Bengal tiger.**

In palaces throughout India, I saw old paintings of maharajas, or rulers, on epic tiger hunts. Even though the hunters usually rode elephants into the jungle to protect themselves and used guns to hunt, killing one of the planet's most powerful animals was a way for men to show off their own strength. A successful hunt usually brought home one or two dead tigers.

As weapons grew more sophisticated, though, one hunter could kill more than 1,000 tigers in a lifetime, Sen said. At the same time, the Indian government decided that

- **What cultural or religious significance do tigers have in India?**

NEWS DETECTIVE   by Emily Sohn

People go on wildlife safaris for all sorts of reasons. For many tourists, the biggest draw is the chance to see exotic creatures that they could never see in the wild at home.

On the drive toward Ranthambore National Park, my friend Annie Feidt explained why she wanted to see a tiger in the wild.

"Because they are fast and powerful and beautiful," she said. After traveling for eight months, Annie also missed her own tiger-like friend at home. "They remind me of my cat Oly, only they are so much bigger and they run really fast. I want to see a baby tiger."

Annie's fiancé Dave Bass liked the element of adventure involved in a tiger safari. "What excites me," he said, "is being somewhere that a tiger could be lurking around any corner."

I was interested in conservation. I knew that tigers are endangered animals, and I wanted to learn something about them. Maybe seeing them would assure me that there is still some "wild" left in India.

When the safari began at around 2:00 P.M., I was optimistic. My eyes darted from one side of the truck to the other. I talked to people, but I refused to look at them. I was afraid I would miss seeing a tiger lurking behind a rock.

After an hour, my mind started to wander. I wondered what kinds of trees I was looking at. I enjoyed the scenery. I took pictures of some of the other wildlife, including monkeys, peacocks, wolves, wild boars, and crocodiles. I started chatting with other passengers.

After two hours, I started to feel skeptical that we would ever see any tigers. The truck was loud. We were driving too fast. I was wearing an orange jacket. There were

other trucks in front of us. Why would a tiger stick around for all that racket?

Then, I started to get cranky. My seat was uncomfortable. The dirt roads were bumpy and rough. As the sun slipped lower in the sky, the temperature dropped, and I started to get cold. I was disappointed that there was no guide to talk to about tigers.

By the time we returned to our hotel, more than three hours after we started, all I wanted was a cup of tea and a hot shower. I decided not to sit through another safari the next morning.

We found out later that we had made the wrong decision. People who came back from the morning safari said they saw three tigers.

I left Ranthambore disappointed. I wanted to see tigers, or at least learn about them. Instead, I got a bumpy ride on a truck that made lots of noise and spewed diesel fumes. If I were a tiger, I probably would have made myself invisible, too.

Erin Bomkamp, a 26-year-old biologist from Orange County, California, who was on my safari, made me feel a little better. "Even if you don't see tigers," she said, "there's lots of other good stuff to see."

To prove the point, her father, Tony, also a biologist, pulled out a book about birds. He had seen more than 100 species of birds during his two days in the park, he said, including the rare and beautiful saurus crane.

I started to think that they were right. Just because I didn't see a tiger didn't mean the safari was a failure. After all, I did get to drive on roads that tigers had crossed and see animals that tigers eat.

Just knowing that tigers were out there was thrilling enough.

tigers were a threat to people and offered rewards for killing them.

"Can you believe that I have seen in my lifetime as little as 20 rupees (that's 40 cents) paid by the government for shooting a tiger," Sen said.

Beginning early in the 20th century, tourists from around the world flocked to India just to shoot tigers. By the late 1960s, however, most visitors couldn't find any. A rough count at that time turned up fewer than 2,000 tigers in all of India.

- **What are the main threats to the tiger population in India?**

LOSING TIGERS

Losing tigers would be an enormous disaster, Sen said. Tigers are important **predators** at the top of a food chain. They play a vital role in India's ecosystems.

Without tigers to keep deer populations in check, for instance, deer would multiply out of control and eat up all the vegetation in an area. That could lead to flooding or soil changes. Silt could fill rivers that people depend on for irrigating their fields.

- **Why is it important to have predators in an ecosystem?**

Losing tigers would also be a shame because the animals are so breathtakingly beautiful and impressive. "If you see a tiger in the wild, you will fall in love," Sen told me, as we sat sipping cups of spicy milk tea. "You'll simply be hypnotized."

"You forget everything when you see a tiger," he said. "Every movement is phenomenal. They are powerful, swift, cunning, smart, charming. They are the most attractive things in the world."

Sen is not alone in his passion for tigers. The animals are now so important to India's national identity that the government started a program called Project Tiger in 1973 to put aside land just for the protection of tigers. Today, there are 27 tiger reserves, covering more than 37,000 square miles [95,830 km^2].

Tigers are thriving inside the reserves. Outside of them, however, things aren't going quite as well. As

• **Describe "Project Tiger."**

human populations grow, conflicts between people and tigers are becoming more common, and tigers usually lose. When tigers attack grazing cattle, for instance, farmers often retaliate by poisoning the cats.

In response, WWF–India is setting up a compensation program in a number of areas around the country. When someone's cow is killed by a tiger, WWF–India will give that person money to make up for the loss and turn him away from taking matters into his own hands. The money comes from donors to WWF–India.

Other organizations are battling the problem of

- **Why has India set up a compensation fund for farmers whose cows are killed by a tiger?**

poaching. Some people illegally kill tigers to sell their valuable bones, furs, and other body parts. The Wildlife Protection Society of India, for one, helps officials nab poachers and seize their wares.

ZOO STORY

Disappointed with my safari and desperate for at least one tiger experience in India, I decided to go to the zoo in New Delhi on my last day in the country. In a fenced-off area, I saw two tigers lying lazily in the sunshine. One looked at me and yawned. The other barely twitched a whisker.

As I was about to leave the zoo to catch my airplane home, I heard a spine-chilling roar. There, behind me, was a giant Bengal tiger pacing fiercely around a small cage. A crowd of people gathered to watch the tiger strut and bare its teeth.

The sight was both magnificent and terrifying. I was glad the cage bars were strong. Maybe I didn't need to see a tiger in the wild after all.

After Reading:

- Why would the tiger, as a symbol of power and strength, become a coveted animal to hunt and kill?

- What predators do you think are missing from the ecosystem around your house?

- Would you be interested in going to India to see a tiger? Why or why not?

- Do you think people should be allowed to hunt wild animals?

- How do you think seeing a tiger in a zoo is different from seeing one in the wild?

- Do you think it's likely that tigers will disappear from Earth?

Endangered Elephants

Many environmentalists and animal rights activists dislike the idea of zoos and circuses. They argue that animals should not be taken captive, but left in their natural habitat. Under ordinary circumstances, it would seem to be better to leave wild animals in the wild. For the endangered Asian elephants, however, zoos and circuses may be the only hope for survival, when their native home is filled with lurking hunters who are more interested in making profits than protecting animals.

—The Editor

Helping to Save Elephants

by Emily Sohn

Before Reading:

- **Have you ever seen an animal show? If so, where was it? What did the animals do? What did the trainer do?**

- **Can an animal "befriend" a person? What evidence would lead you to believe that they were friends?**

- **Jot down some objections people might have to keeping animals in a circus. After reading this article, see which, if any, of your objections were addressed.**

I wouldn't last a minute in the circus.

At a recent exhibit at the Science Museum of Minnesota in St. Paul, I had a chance to try. I stuffed my body into a contortionist's box and almost got stuck. I attempted to walk across a tightrope hanging low to the ground, but I wobbled and fell off after nearly every step. I couldn't even lift the big, heavy stick that acrobats use for balance.

When I left the museum, I was more convinced than ever that the best place for me at a circus is in the audience.

83

If I were an Asian elephant, however, I might consider joining the circus. That's not because the bulky animals have it any easier than the rest of the troupe. In fact, circus elephants train for hours every day to learn their routines. Yet, for endangered Asian elephants, a circus might be a safer place to live than any wild area in Asia.

The Ringling Bros. and Barnum & Bailey® circus, in particular, has been working extra hard in recent years to help keep Asian elephants from dying out (Figure 3.1). At its Center for Elephant Conservation in central Florida, scientists and trainers focus entirely on protecting, breeding, and studying Asian elephants.

"Regardless of what happens in Asia, it's our goal to ensure that the Asian elephant doesn't disappear from the Earth," says animal behaviorist John Kirtland, executive director of animal stewardship at Feld Entertainment, the company that produces the Ringling Bros. circus. "We want to preserve it for our children and our children's children."

FIRST IMPRESSIONS

With elephants, first impressions can be quite impressive. After spending about 22 months inside their mothers' wombs, baby Asian elephants are born weighing an average of 250 pounds [113 kg]. Adult females weigh between 8,000 and 10,000 pounds [between 3,629 and

Figure 3.1 Asian elephants face extreme danger from poachers in their natural habitat.

4,536 kg]. Fully grown males can weigh as much as 12,000 pounds [5,443 kg]. Adults can grow to be 10 feet [3 meters] tall. Males have huge, beautiful ivory tusks.

Preserving such an enormous creature can be an enormous challenge. There are two species of elephants living on Earth today. The species that lives in Africa is threatened, and Asian elephants are in big trouble.

One-fifth of the world's people live in Asia, and their activities are

- **List five interesting facts about the Asian elephant. Make up a multiple-choice test using these questions and see how well your friends and family members do answering your questions.**

squeezing elephants out. Meanwhile, **poachers** are killing males at an alarming rate for their tusks, which sell for lots of money on the **black market**.

Today, there are probably fewer than 35,000 elephants living in the wild in Asia, Kirtland says. That may sound like a big number, but the future looks bleak. For one thing, elephant populations have been split up into small, vulnerable groups. Also, with so few males left, it's hard for elephants to mate efficiently.

In fact, Asian elephants are so threatened now that Kirtland estimates they could disappear in fewer than 20 years. "The Asian elephant is going to go extinct as a wild animal," he says, "because the wild does not exist anymore."

- **What factors are contributing to the decline of Asian elephants in Asia?**

Still, Kirtland and his colleagues at Ringling Bros. want to make sure that the animals don't disappear altogether, even if they remain only in captivity. Ringling Bros. itself has 55 Asian elephants in its herd. At any given time, about half of them are on tour with the circus. The rest hang out at the Center for Elephant Conservation (CEC), where they train, participate in studies, or relax, depending on their stage in life. Ringling Bros. finished building the facility in 1995 on a 200-acre [81-hectare] site between Tampa and Orlando.

MATING IN CAPTIVITY

Altogether, fewer than 100 elephants have been born and bred in the United States in the 200 years since Asian elephants were first brought to the country. Since the early 1990s, Ringling Bros. has bred 16 of the 42 Asian elephants born in North America, equal to the number produced by all the zoos combined.

One of the biggest challenges of maintaining a thriving elephant community is getting the animals to mate in captivity. With practice, scientists have learned some important tricks. "You don't just put a male and female together," says Kirtland.

After working with animals for years, Kirtland believes that a healthy dose of competition is the key for successful courtship. "If you put one guy in a room full of women, he's casual," he says. "Put several guys in a room full of women, they have to compete for the women's attention."

One project is trying to skirt the courtship issue altogether by looking at the possibility of artificial insemination. Researchers are trying lab techniques to fertilize female elephants without mating them. CEC veterinarians also draw blood regularly to see which elephants are pregnant or ready to mate.

By keeping animals in captivity, scientists have had a chance to learn basic things about elephants that wouldn't be possible otherwise. Trained elephants will stand still during uncomfortable medical procedures, for example, allowing researchers to collect general information about their bodies and health.

As part of another, more conservation-minded project, researchers at the Center are studying how elephants perceive smells. They want to find odors that are particularly repulsive to elephants so that they can design "odor fences" that would keep wild elephants from destroying farmers' crops. That might win the animals additional human friends in Asia.

- **What is an "odor fence?"**

FUTURE GENERATIONS

Despite all the research and conservation efforts at the Center, there are still plenty of animal lovers who hate zoos and circuses. They argue that it's not fair to keep exotic animals locked up in artificial environments. Some local governments have even banned animal acts in their towns, fearing that the animals aren't treated well.

Kirtland disagrees with such criticisms. For one thing, circus elephants live longer than zoo elephants or elephants in the wild, he says. In captivity, they can live well into their 60s and 70s. In the wild, a female elephant is lucky to reach 50. Males rarely live longer than 30 years.

The circus has the potential to benefit future generations of elephants, too, Kirtland says. In almost every city the company visits, Ringling Bros. holds an animal open house where ticket-holders can visit the animal compound, talk to the staff, and learn about the animals.

This kind of personal connection can make all the difference, says Kirtland, who saw his first elephant in a circus when he was five or six years old. "For many people, the first or only time they ever see an elephant is when the circus comes to town," he says.

Most people will never get to Africa or Asia on extended safaris. Yet each year, more than 200 million people go to circuses and zoos, Kirtland estimates. Ringling Bros. alone visits within 90 miles [145 km] of more than 90% of the U.S. population. Once people have seen exotic animals, researchers hope, they will be more likely to want to help protect them.

> • **For an Asian elephant, what are the benefits of becoming part of a circus such as Ringling Bros.?**

WORKING WITH HUMANS

Elephants have a long history of relationships with humans. For thousands of years, people have been using the animals to help with agriculture, logging, and military activities. Elephants have also taken on important roles in mythology and religion. Ancient religions in India, South

China, Sri Lanka, and elsewhere have featured gods that had elephant heads.

There's plenty to admire. Elephant cultures are complex, and the animals are surprisingly smart. They can learn to respond to more than 60 vocal commands. And they seem to form friendships with their trainers.

At least, the trainers seem to think so. "Our elephants are part of our family as much as our human partners are," Kirtland says. "We've all missed holidays, family gatherings, and birthdays because the needs of our animals come first."

Elephant-like animals have lived on Earth for more than 55 million years, far longer than we have. It's perhaps this sense of majesty that drives Kirtland and many of his colleagues to work so hard at saving them. "They are magnificent animals," Kirtland says. "A world without elephants would be a much sadder place."

After Reading:

- What is the main question this article answers?

- An elephant can respond to more than 60 vocal commands. What are the first three commands you would teach an elephant to respond to?

- If you had $100,000 to donate to help save Asian elephants, how would you ask that that money be spent?

- Is it really important to save the Asian elephant? Why?

- When herds of animals become small, genetic inbreeding often occurs. What problems might genetic inbreeding cause?

- The elephant is an impressive animal. Is it also important to save less impressive animals? Explain.

Section 4

Pollution

When you think of environmental issues, pollution is likely the first thing that comes to mind. It's no wonder. If you live near any major city, you've probably seen huge smokestacks billowing with foul-looking fumes or mountains of garbage stored in landfills because it can't be broken down and disposed of easily. Pollution is one of the most pressing threats to the Earth—and one of the issues we can do something about. In this section, we look at some sources of pollution, their effects on the environment, and the steps being taken to try to stop the damage pollution is doing.

In the first article, author Emily Sohn describes an unusual source of pollution: dust falling from the sky. The second article explores the problem of pollution associated with detergents and the strange irony of how we are polluting the Earth while we get ourselves clean. The third article talks about an exciting new idea for cleaning up contaminated soil—using tiny sponge-like particles that soak up pollutants. Finally, author Emily Sohn shows how bacteria—the same organisms that can cause disease in people—may be extremely useful for breaking down pollutants and cleaning up the Earth.

—The Editor

Dust in the Wind

Sky dust isn't quite the same thing as the grime that settles on your furniture at home. Instead, it's tiny bits of material that come from outer space—pieces of comets and asteroids that you probably don't even notice. Although sky dust, like any other kind of dust, can be a pollutant, it can also help scientists learn more about the universe. In the next article, author Emily Sohn explores the use of sky dust to make discoveries about weather, outer space, and—the topic of this section—pollution.

—The Editor

Sky Dust Keeps Falling on Your Head

by Emily Sohn

Before Reading:

- Dust makes you cough and sneeze, so why might scientists think it's worth sticking their noses into that topic?

- Where might dust come from in the first place?

Any time you go outside, you get pummeled by invisible storms of dust. Even on a perfectly sunny day, you inhale pieces of dead bugs. Floating specks of hair and pollen settle on your skin. Tiny chunks of comets might even fall on your head from outer space.

"Every time you sit on a bench, you're sitting on cosmic dust," says astronomer Don Brownlee from the University of Washington in Seattle. In fact, 6 million pounds [2.7 million kg] of space dust settle on the planet every year, he says. "If you're outside during the day, you're probably going to get hit by a couple of things."

You might never notice the stuff falling all around you. But some scientists collect cosmic dust and other kinds of floating particles to learn about weather patterns, pollution, and the origin of the universe.

DOWN TO EARTH

And now a new project is bringing sky dust studies down to Earth: Maybe someday soon even you can help.

Studies of outer space have traditionally involved lots of expensive equipment. Brownlee and his colleagues, for example, send hi-tech airplanes more than 65,000 feet [19,812 meters] above Earth's surface. The aircraft fly at three-quarters the speed of sound for 50 hours or so, collecting cosmic dust on a sterile filter about the size of a deck of cards.

About half of what they pick up are micrometeorites—pieces of comets and asteroids about as wide as a human hair is thick. Back on Earth, the scientists analyze the space dust as a window into the past.

Meteorites are the only records we have of the origin of the universe, Brownlee says. "They date back in time to when the sun and Earth formed 4 1/2 billion years ago."

Hoping to get an even clearer view of that history, Brownlee's team has sent a spacecraft called *Stardust* to collect samples from a comet for the first time. . . .

It will be the first mission to collect material from space since astronauts brought moon rocks back in 1972.

Brownlee hopes the *Stardust* mission will bring back useful information about our own planet, too.

"The Earth was 100 percent made from things that came in from space," Brownlee says. "By looking at things that are still in space, we can look at things that participated in the formation of the Earth."

BLOWING IN THE WIND

But we can learn just as much by looking at what's already here, says Dan Murray, a geologist at the University of Rhode Island. His new project invites kids, teachers, and other interested people to contribute to a worldwide study of everything that's blowing in the wind, including cosmic dust.

Along with Jim Sammons, a retired high school science teacher, Murray is gathering a network of sites around the world, where people will collect samples of sky dust, analyze it, and send their results to a public Website: *http://www.skydust.org/*.

Sky dust can reveal all sorts of interesting things about global weather patterns and pollution, Murray says.

• **What kinds of information might skillful detectives find in the dust that's circulating thousands of miles above Earth?**

In Rhode Island, for example, the researchers have collected Mongolian dust that drifted all the way across the Atlantic Ocean. In another case, kids who lived east of Lake Michigan traced twice-monthly onslaughts of carbon soot back to pollution-spitting barges on the lake.

Collecting sky dust is easy, Murray says. First, you line an inflatable kids' swimming pool with a certain kind of waterproof, windproof fabric and leave it out in the open for 48 hours. Then, you use special crime-scene tape to pick up whatever has settled and put the tape in a beaker of water to dissolve.

With just a basic microscope, a good guidebook, and a little practice, anyone can tell the difference between different kinds of dust, pollen, even micrometeorites, Murray says. A fancier microscope reveals even more details.

If enough schools sent in data about the kinds of bugs, pollen, and other particles falling in their area, they might be able to help scientists track pollution, predict buggy seasons, measure meteor showers, or detect signs of global climate change.

EARTH'S HEALTH

Those are all important clues about the overall health of the planet, Murray says. "Kids across the country could become the early-warning systems for looking for things that might not be good that are happening to this or that part of the planet."

And while the *Stardust* mission is expensive and far away, the Skydust project will give real kids the chance to do real science.

"You don't really know the answers, and that's the exciting thing," Murray says.

Jim Sammons agrees: "Just throw away the textbook, and right away the horizon becomes clear."

After Reading:

- **What new sources of dust did you learn about by reading this article?**

- **What advantages do we, as students here on Earth, have over even the most complex instruments used by astronauts in space programs? What can these instruments explore that we never could study by ourselves?**

- **If you wanted to collect dust samples, what tools might you use? Design a simple system. Try it out! Look at the Website *http://www.skydust.org* .**

- **Do you recommend spending school time on a project collecting and analyzing dust? Why or why not?**

Damaging Detergents

Everybody knows it's important to be clean to stay healthy. Every day, we wash our bodies, our dishes, and our homes. But what gets us clean and rids us of potentially harmful bacteria can actually hurt other living things. The soaps and detergents we use end up as chemical runoff in the environment, where they can cause terrible harm to algae and other living things.

—The Editor

The Down Side of Keeping Clean

by Emily Sohn

Wash your hands. Brush your teeth. Scrub the toilet. Do the dishes. Being clean is supposed to keep us healthy by destroying **bacteria** that make us sick.

But our meticulous attention to cleanliness might have a down side. New research suggests that the chemicals we use to clean and disinfect could be damaging the environment by killing off algae at the base of the food chain.

Over the past decade, the war against bacteria has been escalating. From dish soap to toothpaste, cleaning products have become increasingly deadly to the tiny troublemakers. After getting dumped down the drain, those household chemicals usually go straight through the sewer system and into lakes and streams, ignored by wastewater treatment plants.

Curious about the environmental effects of all that chemical runoff, environmental scientist Brittan A. Wilson of the University of Kansas in Lawrence and colleagues collected algae from a Kansas stream. In the lab, the scientists doused the algae with three common household chemicals in concentrations comparable to levels often found in American streams.

The number of species of algae and overall growth of algae dropped in samples treated with the chemicals, but not in untreated samples, the researchers report.

Those results may be alarming, but they shouldn't be a complete surprise. "It's stupid to think that chemicals that keep toothpaste safe from bacteria won't have an effect at the other end of the sewer pipe," says ecologist Stanley I. Dodson of the University of Wisconsin-Madison. What is surprising is that even low concentrations of the chemicals can have a big effect.

Going Deeper:

Morgan, Kendall. "Clean Casualties: Everyday Chemicals May Shift Ecosystems." *Science News* 163 (March 29, 2003): 196. Available online at *http://www.sciencenews.org/20030329/fob3.asp*.

A Tiny Clean-up Crew

You've probably used a sponge to clean up messes in the kitchen. Imagine if your sponge was too small for you to see with the naked eye. It would be pretty useless, you might think. But you'd be wrong. As author Emily Sohn explains in the following article, scientists have found a very good use for microscopic particles that act as sponges—soaking up pollution and turning it into harmless chemicals that pose no threat to the environment.

—The Editor

Nanosponges Soak up Pollutants

by Emily Sohn

What could be worse than toxic sludge seeping into soil, poisoning animals and people? The headache of cleaning up all that muck.

For years, engineers have struggled to get oil and tar out of the ground at hazardous-waste sites around the United States. Current methods are costly and inefficient.

Now, environmental engineers from Cornell University say they may have a better solution. Their strategy involves **nanotechnology**, a new type of science involving very, very tiny things.

In this case, the researchers created a special type of particle, measuring just 20 **nanometers** across. In comparison, each hair on your head is about 50,000 nanometers wide. The surface of the particle attracts water. The inside avoids water.

The engineers then pumped a solution containing the new particles into a column of sand that was contaminated with a chemical called phenanthrene. The chemical is often found in coal tar.

The nanoparticles were small enough to move through spaces between the sand grains. As the particles moved upward from the bottom of the sand column, their

Storm Water and Aquatic Communities

Ecotoxicology of Stormwater Pollution in Our Aquatic Communities
David J. Marash-Whitman, 12, Saratoga, California
National Park Service Explorer Team Award, Discovery Channel Young Scientist Challenge, 2004

Project background: David was horrified to find out that storm water runoff from houses, cars, and farms near his home dumps directly into a nearby bay. He wanted to know if pollutants in this water hampered the growth of organisms.

Tactics and results: David chose nine residential pollutants, including pool cleaners, auto maintenance fluids, paint thinner, pesticides, and herbicides. He exposed lettuce seeds to low concentrations of the pollutants over five days. He also grew lettuce seeds in storm water samples.

David found that copper algaecide, a pool cleaner, was most toxic. Seeds grown in the presence of other pollutants also failed to thrive. Seeds grown in storm water fared worse than seeds grown in clean water.

water-hating interiors sucked phenanthrene out of the sand, trapping it inside.

The next challenge is to figure out how to make sure the cleanser nanoparticles return to the surface of the soil, where they can be gathered up and flushed clean of chemicals.

To get around that problem, another group of scientists is trying to make nanoparticles that can convert contaminants into less harmful chemicals. That way, the particles could just stay in the soil.

Smaller may really be better when it comes to cleaning up contaminated soil.

Going Deeper:

Goho, Alexandra. "Nanosponges: Plastic Particles Pick up Pollutants." *Science News* 165 (February 21, 2004): 116–117. Available online at *http://www.sciencenews.org/articles/20040221/fob4.asp*.

Information for kids about soil contamination can be found online at *www.epa.gov/superfund/students/wastsite/soilspil.htm*.

Helpful Bacteria

When you hear the word *bacteria*, you probably think of the organisms that sometimes cause diseases that range from strep throat to bacterial meningitis. But not all bacteria are harmful. In fact, some—like those that live in our guts—are quite helpful because they "eat up" chemicals and other materials that could pose a threat to us. The same idea holds true when it comes to pollution. As author Emily Sohn shows in the next article, scientists have discovered that certain types of bacteria can play a vital role in cleaning up toxic waste.

—The Editor

Toxic Cleanups Get a Microbe Boost

by Emily Sohn

Garbage can be a huge problem. It not only stinks and takes up space but also can be hazardous to your health. Toxic waste can seep into the soil and pollute the environment.

Now, researchers from Cornell University have come up with a technique to help clean up toxic-waste sites. They think bacteria in the soil might help.

The idea is to find microbes that naturally break down specific toxic chemicals. To test their strategy, the scientists went to a coal tar waste site belonging to a factory that once converted coal into gas. The waste included a chemical known as naphthalene, the main ingredient of moth balls. They marked a sample of naphthalene with a special atomic label so they could recognize it later and added it to the soil.

The researchers wanted to find out if there were tiny microbes in the soil that could break down naphthalene on their own. So, they put glass jars on top of different patches of soil. If microbes were breaking down naphthalene, the jars would fill with carbon dioxide gas marked with the same label the scientists had used to mark the ingredient. That would show where in the soil

Effect of Skyglow on Star Visibility

Quantifying the Effect of Skyglow on the Visibility of Stars
Jacob Rucker, 13, Del Mar, California
Discovery Kids "TV Star" Award, Discovery Channel Young
Scientist Challenge, 2003

Project background: Skyglow, caused by excess light from urban centers, reduces the visibility of stars and is an increasing problem for astronomical observations. Jacob lives in the San Diego area, where the climate is dry, the skies are clear, and mountains loom nearby—ideal conditions for night-sky observations. However, light pollution in this area hampers visibility at the Palomar Observatory and Mount Laguna Observatory. Jacob wanted to test whether it was possible to predict the impact of skyglow based on a site's distance from an urban center.

Tactics and results: From sites 30, 60, 75, and 124 kilometers [19, 37, 47, and 77 miles] from the urban center of San Diego County, Jacob took 120 photographs of the zenith on nights of similar weather and moonlight conditions between August 2002 and January 2003. He developed and scanned the photos, turning them into more than 500 bitmap files. Then, he wrote a computer program to convert the bitmap files into pixel arrays, with pixel intensity values ranging from 0 to 765, and to determine the number of pixels at each intensity level. He used the intensity intervals for each site to find the change in intensity (brightness) as a function of a site's distance from the urban center.

Using the formula he developed, Jacob found that the observable, visible light from stars remains below 50% until about 35 kilometers from a city the size of San Diego. The visibility does not improve to 90% until you reach a distance of 70 kilometers away from the city. Thus, skyglow is a serious threat to astronomical observations at Mount Laguna Observatory (45 miles [72 km] from San Diego) and Palomar Observatory (40 miles [64 km] from San Diego).

the helpful bacteria lived. They could then look for those bacteria.

The researchers now hope to find bacteria that break down cancer-causing pollutants in coal tar. If it works out, bacteria could become important helpers for cleaning up dangerous chemical messes.

Going Deeper:

Goho, Alexandra. "Toxic Cleanups Get a Boost." *Science News* 164 (November 22, 2003): 333. Available online at *http://www.sciencenews.org/20031122/note10.asp*.

You can learn more about toxic waste cleanups at *www.epa.gov/superfund/kids/*.

bacteria: Single-celled organisms that may cause disease.

black market: Illegal system of trade.

diatoms: Tiny single-celled forms of algae.

ecologist: A scientist who studies the relationships between living things and their environment.

ecosystems: Communities of organisms and their environments.

estuaries: Branches of the sea found at the lower end of a river.

food chain: An arrangement of living things within a particular ecosystem, in which organisms are placed in order of the kinds of food they eat, with those that produce their own food (such as plants) on the bottom, and predators that eat other animals at higher levels.

fossil fuels: Coal, oil, or natural gas produced in the Earth from the remains of plants or animals.

geology: The study of the history of the Earth and its living things, as recorded in rocks.

global warming: A gradual increase in the temperature of the Earth.

green: Not harmful to the environment.

greenhouse gases: Components of the atmosphere that contribute to global warming; the major greenhouse gases include water vapor, carbon dioxide, and ozone.

habitats: Places in which particular plants or animals typically live.

infrared: Refers to radiation that has a wavelength between 700 nanometers and 1 millimeter.

larvae: The immature, wingless forms that hatch from the eggs of many insects.

microorganisms: Living things that are too small to be seen without the aid of a microscope.

nanometers: Units of measurement equal to one-billionth of a meter.

nanotechnology: The building of microscopic devices.

nutrias: Large South American rodents with webbed hind feet and a nearly hairless tail.

plankton: Tiny animals or plants that float or swim weakly in water environments.

poachers: People who illegally kill or take wild animals.

predators: Animals that feed on other animals.

satellite: A man-made or natural object that orbits a planet in space.

sediment: The matter that settles at the bottom of a liquid.

solar cells: Devices that collect energy from the sun for use as a power source.

West Nile virus: Disease spread by mosquitoes that can cause encephalitis and death in both birds and humans.

Further Reading

Books

Beil, Karen Magnuson. *Fire in Their Eyes: Wildfires and the People Who Fight Them*. Orlando, FL: Harcourt, 1999.

Burnie, David. *Earth Watch*. New York: Dorling Kindersley, 2001.

Johnson, Rebecca L. *A Journey Into a Wetland*. Minneapolis: Carolrhoda Books/Lerner Publications, 2004.

Silverstein, Alvin, Laura Silverstein Nunn, and Virginia Silverstein. *Global Warming*. Minneapolis: Twenty-first Century Books/Millbrook Press, 2003.

Welsbacher, Anne. *Life in a Rain Forest*. Minneapolis: Lerner Publishing, 2003.

Websites

Alliance to Save Energy
http://www.ase.org/

American Cetacean Society
http://www.acsonline.org/

Center for Elephant Conservation
http://www.ringling.com/cec/

Defenders of Wildlife: Northern Spotted Owl
http://www.kidsplanet.org/factsheets/
    northspotowl.html

National Wetlands Research Center
http://www.nwrc.usgs.gov/

Tiger Trust
http://www.indiantiger.com/trust/

U.S. Environmental Protection Agency
http://www.epa.gov/

Wildfires
http://www.fema.gov/kids/bre nner.htm

Yellowstone National Park
http://www.nps.gov/yell/technical/fire/ecology.htm

Trademarks

page:

Contributors

EMILY SOHN is a freelance journalist, based in Minneapolis. She covers mostly science and health for national magazines, including *U.S. News & World Report*, *Health*, *Smithsonian*, and *Science News*. Emily divides her time between writing for kids and writing for adults, and assignments have sent her to countries around the world, including Cuba, Peru, and Sweden. When she's not working, Emily spends most of her time rock climbing, camping, swimming, exploring, and pursuing adventures outdoors.

TARA KOELLHOFFER earned her degree in political science and history from Rutgers University. Today, she is a freelance writer and editor with ten years of experience working on nonfiction books for young adults, covering topics that range from social studies and biography to health and science. She has edited hundreds of books and teaching materials, including a history of Italy published by Greenhaven Press. She lives in Pennsylvania with her husband, Gary, and their dog and cat.